21ˢᵗ
Century
Junior
Library

Responsibility

by Lucia Raatma

CHERRY LAKE PUBLISHING * ANN ARBOR, MICHIGAN

CHERRY LAKE
Publishing

Published in the United States of America by Cherry Lake Publishing
Ann Arbor, Michigan
www.cherrylakepublishing.com

Content Adviser: David Wangaard, Executive Director, SEE: The School for Ethical Education, Milford, Connecticut

Reading Adviser: Marla Conn, ReadAbility, Inc.

Photo Credits: Cover, ©iStockphoto.com/ParkerDeen; page 4, ©Mamahoohooba/Dreamstime.com; page 6, ©iStockphoto.com/peanut8481; page 8, ©bikeriderlondon/Shutterstock, Inc.; page 10, ©Sonya Etchison/Dreamstime.com; page 12, ©ZouZou/Shutterstock, Inc.; page 14, ©iStockphoto.com/DepthofField; page 16, ©iStockphoto.com/robcruse; page 18, ©Nancy Catherine Walker/Shutterstock, Inc.; page 20, ©iStockphoto.com/Kemter.

LIBRARY OF CONGRESS CATALOGING-IN-PUBLICATION DATA

Raatma, Lucia.
  Responsibility/by Lucia Raatma.
     pages cm.—(Character education) (21st century junior library)
  Includes bibliographical references and index.
  ISBN 978-1-62431-157-4 (lib. bdg.)—ISBN 978-1-62431-223-6 (e-book)—
ISBN 978-1-62431-289-2 (pbk.)
  1. Responsibility—Juvenile literature. I. Title.
  BJ1451.R24 2013
  179'.9—dc23   2013004931

Cherry Lake Publishing would like to acknowledge the work of
The Partnership for 21st Century Skills.
Please visit www.p21.org for more information.

Printed in the United States of America
Corporate Graphics Inc.
July 2013
CLFA13

CONTENTS

Be responsible by getting your homework and chores done before playing.

What Is Responsibility?

Greg called his friend Pat and asked if he wanted to come over and play video games.

"I can't right now," said Pat. "I have to clean my room and do my homework first."

"Wow," said Greg. "You sure are responsible!"

Take responsibility for the mistakes you make.

When you are responsible, you are **reliable**. People can count on you. You do what you say you are going to do. You don't expect others to do your work.

Donna is responsible. She owns up to her mistakes. She doesn't blame other people. If she breaks something, she **admits** it. If she forgets to meet her friend Eddie after school, she apologizes.

Do a good job on your chores and get them done on time.

Being Responsible

There are many ways to be responsible. When you tell someone you are going to do something, be sure to do it correctly. Make sure you get it done on time.

Create!

Ask a parent to help you make a chore chart. List all of the chores you are responsible for each week. Check off the tasks as you finish them. That way, you won't forget anything.

Caring for a pet is a lot of responsibility.

Being responsible means thinking before you act. It means keeping in mind how your actions may affect others.

Noah forgot to take his dog outside in the morning. The dog might not get to go to the bathroom if no one is home during the day. Rita forgot to bring her sick friend his homework **assignment** from school. He might not have time to get his work done.

You are responsible for learning the information your teacher gives you.

There are many ways to be responsible at school. Bruce shows responsibility by listening in class. He always finishes his assignments on time. He also follows the rules at school.

Ask Questions!

Are you confused about an assignment? Ask questions! Be sure you understand what you are supposed to do. Teachers will be happy to help you. Asking questions can help you do the best job you can on assignments.

Raising money for charity is a great way to show responsibility in your community.

Being Responsible in Your Community

Everyone plays a part in making the world a better place. You can be responsible by **volunteering**. Make volunteering a family event. Find something that is important to you and your parents. Then find out what you can do to help. Maybe you can all hold a fund-raiser to make money for people in need.

Everyone is responsible for helping to take care of the planet.

You can also be responsible by caring about your **environment**. Patrick is responsible because he doesn't litter. He **recycles** bottles, cans, and paper.

Think! What would happen if people weren't responsible? What if your parents forgot to go to work? What if your teachers forgot to teach you? What would the world be like if people didn't do the things they are supposed to do?

It is irresponsible to leave things where they might get in other people's way.

Another way to be responsible is to help out in your neighborhood. Joanna cleans up after her pets when they make a mess. She doesn't leave her toys lying around in the street or on the sidewalk. They could get in people's way.

If you are responsible, people will know that you are reliable and trustworthy.

When you are responsible, people know they can trust you. They know they can count on you to do what you have promised. Being responsible is good for you. It is also good for all the people around you!

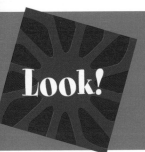

Look!

Who is the most responsible person you know?
Pay attention to the things he or she does.
What can you do to be as responsible as him or her?

GLOSSARY

admits (ad-MITS) agrees that something is true; confesses to something

assignment (uh-SINE-muhnt) job that is given to certain people to do; homework given to you by a teacher is an assignment

environment (en-VYE-ruhn-muhnt) the world around you, including the land, sea, and air

recycles (ree-SYE-kuhlz) processes old items so they can be used to make new products

reliable (ri-LYE-uh-buhl) describing someone whom others can depend on and trust

volunteering (vol-uhn-TIHR-ing) offering to do a job for no pay

FIND OUT MORE

BOOKS

Donahue, Jill L., and Mary Small. *Way To Be!: How to be Brave, Responsible, Honest, and an All-Around Great Kid*. Mankato, MN: Picture Window Books, 2011.

Suen, Anastasia. *Don't Forget! A Responsibility Story*. Edina, MN: Magic Wagon, 2009.

WEB SITES

PBS Kids—Making Money: Responsibility
http://pbskids.org/itsmylife/money /making/article6.html
Learn about ways to be responsible when it comes to working and earning money.

PBS Kids—Pets: Pet Responsibilities
http://pbskids.org/itsmylife /family/pets/article3.html
Read more about what it takes to be a responsible pet owner.

INDEX

ABOUT THE AUTHOR

Lucia Raatma has written dozens of books for young readers. They are about famous people, historical events, ways to stay safe, and other topics. She lives in Florida's Tampa Bay area with her husband and their two children.